The Coming of The Lion of Judah:

25 Daily Advent Devotions

The Messiah from Heaven to earth:

From the First Adam to the Last:

Genesis 1 to the 4 Gospels (in 31 Days)

DEDICATION:

I dedicate this book to:

Every person in the world,
who has kept going, despite 'trials & tribulations.'

I pray you may keep or renew your faith & hope in Almighty God, your Father in heaven, through Jesus His Son; with whom, nothing is impossible.

Psalm 30 v 5:
"Weeping (sadness, feeling overwhelmed) may last for the night.
However:
Joy **will** come in the morning: Happiness
                                                      Triumph
                                                      Singing

May you find renewed hope and encouragement again in the true story of "The Nativity"; this Christmas and always.

The Lord God bless and keep you,
He makes His face shine on you and gives you His PEACE .

In the world you may have troubles , but be encouraged; I have overcome the world . (John 16 v 33)

Introduction

This book tells the story of the Coming of the Lion of Judah from Heaven to earth-
Who is also, the Son of God and the Son of man (people).

It starts at the very beginning of it all…

And then follows comprehensively through history,
the full Genealogy of the promised Messiah, Lion of Judah, from Day 1.

From Genesis 1 v 1, up to all 4 Gospels;
Comprehensively combining Matthew, Mark, Luke & John's version of these true events; all in chronological order.

A great book for Advent readings:
25 Days + extra Daily readings. Total of 31 Days.

It also includes the English meaning of each Hebrew or Greek name.

I have used the YLT Bible, KJV, WEB and original Greek/ Hebrew translations of Scripture.

Abbreviations:
OT: Old Testament (Old Covenant) ;
NT: New Testament (New Covenant)

Colours:

Royal light blue:
The early combined Genealogy of the Messiah up to David
The ongoing Family history of Joseph (His father on earth)
Royal purple: The Genealogy of Mary, Mother of the Messiah from David

Royal dark blue represents God.(Yahweh)

The Holy Spirit in orange.

Christ's words & important messages or happenings, in red.

Luke's Letter to Theophilus

(Luke 1 v 1-4)

In as much as many (people) undertook to write an account concerning the things that had been accomplished amongst us,

As was passed on to us by those who were eyewitnesses from the start and ministers (servants) of the Word,

It seemed good to me too,
having been acquainted with everything from the beginning,

to write to you, accurately (diligently/ carefully) and consecutively, most noble Theophilus

So that you may know the certainty of the teaching (logon/ words), concerning in which you were taught/ instructed.

1 December

The Beginning of the Good News of Jesus Christ, Son of God

(Mark 1 v 1)

The WORD (Logos)

In the beginning the Word was (existed) -
And the Word was with God, and the Word was God.

He was at the beginning with God.

Everything came into existence through Him-
Not even one thing that exists, came into being, without Him.

Life was (is) in Him- this Life was (is) the Light of people.

The Light shines in the darkness, the darkness did not (and cannot) overcome it.
(John 1 v 1-5)

CREATION

In the Beginning, God (Elohim - Father, Son & Holy Spirit)) created the heavens and the earth.

The earth was formless & void & darkness was over the face of the deep

Then The Spirit of God was hovering over the face of the water and God said:

" Let there be Light!" **And there was Light.**

God saw that the Light was good-
so He separated **the Light** from **the darkness.** (Genesis 1 v 1-3)

The 6 days of God's creation

(Genesis 1)

Evening came and then morning, the First day:

Day 1 Light
Day 2 Sky
Day 3 Dry land, sea, vegetation (seed-bearing plants & fruit)
Day 4 Sun, moon, stars
Day 5 Seacreatures,fish, birds
Day 6 Land animals*
Day 7 REST (Set apart as holy - Sabbath in OT (Old Covenant) times,
Sunday in NT (New Covenant)   (Genesis 2 v 1-3)

God saw all that He had created was very good. (Gen 1 v 31)

* Then God said:

 " Let us create man in our image, in our likeness-
they will rule over creation. (Gen 1 v 26,27)

2 December

Creating Adam

The Lord God formed the (first) man

- Out of the dust from the ground and
- Breathed the Breath of Life into his nose, and the man became a living being. (Gen 2 v 7)

Then the Lord God said: " It is not good for man to be alone, I will make him a helper, a suitable 'counterpart'."

(Balances, matches each other emotionally, mentally, life goals-compliments each other in the relationship)
(Gen 2 v 18 YLT)

Creating Eve

The Lord God caused a deep sleep to come over Adam -
While the man was sleeping, God took one of his ribs and covered the area with flesh.

Then the Lord God made the rib which He had taken from the man, into a woman
and brought her to the man (Adam).

The man said:

" This one, at last, is bone of my bone & flesh of my flesh;

She will be called 'woman', because she was taken from 'man'.

This is why a man leaves his father & mother, and bonds with his wife
and they become one flesh
They were both naked, but did not feel ashamed.
(Gen 2 v 21-25)

Therefore God created man in His own image,

He created them male & female.

And He blessed them.

He called them mankind when He had created them.
(Gen 1 v 27, 5 v 2)

God instructed them to multiply and gave them dominion over creation.
 (Gen 1 v 28-30)

Adam called His wife's name Eve- she would be mother of all the living.

So God's first son on earth was called Adam, and God's first daughter on
earth was called Eve.

Adam means: Man, earth, ground
                (Because God had made Him from the dust of the earth).
Eve means: Giving life (She would bring children into the world).

God said to them :
 " I give you every plant on the entire surface of the earth that has seed
& every tree that brings fruit from its seed as food for you . "
(Genesis 1 v 29; and see the change; after the flood in Gen 9 v 3, 4)

The Garden of Eden

The Lord God (aka Yahweh)) had planted a garden in the East, in Eden
and there He placed the man, whom He had created -

To work it and watch over it.

The Lord God made all kinds of trees grow from the ground -
trees pleasant to look at and good for food

In the middle of the garden stood:

- The tree of Life
- The tree of knowledge of good and evil

A river from Eden watered the garden.
(This divided into 4 rivers - 2 of which are called Tigris & Euphrates even
today)

The Lord God commanded
(because He is God, and knows what is best for us):

" You are free to eat from any tree of the garden;

But,

You must not eat from the tree of knowledge of good and evil-
on the day you eat from it, you will certainly die.
                              (Gen 2 v 8-17)

3 December

Snake:

The Snake (satan; the devil) was the most cunning of all the wild animals.

The Snake to the woman (Eve):

"Did God indeed say that you are not allowed to eat from any of the trees in the garden?"

The woman:

"We may eat from the fruit of the trees of the garden,
but of the fruit of the tree in the middle of the garden -
God said that we must not eat from or touch or we shall die."

The snake:

"You will surely not die,
God knows that when you eat from it, your eyes will be opened ,
and you will be like God- knowing good from evil" (Distinguishing between the two)
(Gen 3 v 1-5)

Sin:

The woman saw that the tree was good for food, pleasant to look at and DESIRABLE to make one 'wise' -

She took of its fruit and ate it;
and she also gave some to her husband with her, and he ate .

So their eyes were opened and they knew that they were naked.

So they sewed together some fig leaves & made coverings for themselves.

In the breeze of the day,

they heard the sound of Yahweh , God (Elohim) , walking in the garden

And Adam & his wife,
hid themselves from the presence of Yahweh God (Elohim),
among the trees of the garden. (Gen 3 v 6-8)

Suffering:

God Yahweh, Elohim called & spoke: "Adam, where are you."

Adam:
"I heard your voice in the garden and I was afraid (scared) ,
because I was naked, and I hid myself."

God:
" Who told you that you are naked;
did you eat from the tree that I had commanded you, not to eat from?"

Adam:
The woman you gave me, she gave me of the fruit and I ate it.

God (Yahweh, Elohim) to the woman:

" What is this that you have done.":

The woman (Eve): "The Snake deceived me and I ate."

God to the snake:

"Because you have done this, you are cursed (you shall sail on your
belly and eat dust all your life).

And I will put enmity between you and the woman;
and between your seed and her Seed- (you shall bruise his heel only)

He will crush (demolish) your head." (Gen 3 v 5)

Consequences of sin:

God to Eve :

Giving birth will be painful… (Gen 3 v 16)

God to Adam:

The ground is cursed and will produce thorns; In the sweat of your face you shall eat bread, until you return to the ground.

(Gen 3 v 17-19)

They had to leave the Garden of Eden, which was from then on guarded by a Guardian angel with a flaming sword. (Gen 3 v 9 -24)

Solution:

God's Promise of The **MESSIAH:**

And I will put enmity between you and the woman;
and between your seed and her Seed-
He will crush (demolish) your head (you shall bruise his heel only)

(Gen 3 v 15)

4 December

Cain & Abel ~ Seth

So now , on earth,

GOD had:

A son called Adam (man, ground, earth) &
A daughter called Eve (life, gives life).

Adam knew his wife intimately , she conceived,
and gave birth to CAIN and some time after, to Abel.

Cain

- Means: Acquired

(Eve said: " I have had; acquired a male child, with the help of the Lord.")

- Cultivated the land
- Presented some of the produce to the Lord

Abel

- Means: Fleeting, a breath
- A shepherd of flock
- Brought some of the firstborn of his flock & their fat to God

Yahweh (God) looked favourably on Abel's offer , had respect for it;
but not the same for Cain; so

Cain was furious

The Lord to Cain:

" Why are you furious and downcast
You will also be accepted if you do well;
and if not- Be aware: Sin is at your door, and it desires to rule over you;
however, you must rule over it. (Gen 4 v7)

In spite of this warning, from the Lord God (Yahweh) Himself,
Cain soon after tricked and invited Abel to go out into the fields, and he
killed him there.

The Lord God to Cain: "Your brother's blood is crying out to me."

Yahwed (God) cursed the ground that Cain would work, but had mercy
in that He spared his life. (Genesis 4 v 1- 24)

Seth

At age 130, Adam & Eve had Seth

Seth

•Means: Appointed; placed; 'substitute'
(Eve said: " God has given me another child, in the place of Abel.")
•Looked a lot like Adam (in his image)

(Adam lived 930 years, and had more sons & daughters)
                                        (Gen 5 v 1-6)

5 December

Seth to Enoch

Seth (at age 105) & his wife had a son called:

Enosh (Frailty)

At this time, people started to call on the Name of the Lord (Gen 4 v 26).

His son was:

Cainan (humble) whose son was:

Mahaleel (Splendour of God, Rising Brightness), had a son:

Jared (Descent) who had Enoch.

ENOCH walked with God, and…

- Means Dedicated, Trained, Disciplined

- At age 65 had Methuselah:

From then on Enoch walked with God for many years (300)

- Then He was not to be found, because God took him home with Him.
- Enoch is also commended for his faith in Hebrews 11.

- From his descendants, Enoch became the Great-grandfather of Noah

Enoch to Noah

Enoch had a son called:

Methuselah
(Man of sword, lived 969 years) who had a son:

Lamech
(Wild, Strong youth, Strike down) who had a son:

NOAH
(Rest- may God give us rest from our hard labour, working the earth)

(Genesis 5)

In these times there were also gigantic people (Nepilim- see Gen 6)
When mankind had multiplied, God decided to reduce the years on earth of people, to 120 years
(Gen. 6 v 3)

The earth(most people) were corrupt & filled with violence;
their every thought and inclination were evil. (Gen 6 v 11,12)

But for NOAH:

Who found grace in the eyes of Yahweh. (God)

6 December

Noah

- A righteous man (& preached the same- 2 Peter 2 v 5)
- He walked 'habitually' with the Lord (YLT)
- Had 3 sons: Shem, Ham, Japheth
(Genesis 6)

The earth was corrupt before God, and was full of violence;
      all flesh were corrupt-
So God said to Noah that He was going to destroy it all (through excess rain and water) and that Noah had to build an Ark.
(to save himself , his wife and children; and pairs of each animal).

"I am going to put an end to all people, because the earth is filled with violence and corruption because of them.
I am surely going to destroy both them and the earth, so make yourself an ark. (Gen 6 v 9-22)

But I will establish my covenant with you, and you & your family must go into the ark." (Gen 6 v 18)

- Noah ~ Did everything the Lord told Him to do.
      (Gen 6 v 22; Gen 7 v 5)

By faith Noah acted with Godly fear,
 having been warned Divinely of things that were not yet visible.
He prepared the Ark and saved his household, by which he condemned the world and became heir of righteousness through faith. (Hebrews 11 v 7)

The ark

Built by God's instructions, eg had a window, coated to be waterproof
Big enough for Noah's wife, 3 sons and their 3 wives
Animals (male & female pair), food
Noah was 500 years when he started to build and entered when he was
600 years old
(took around 100 years to build) (Genesis 6)

God waited patiently for people to repent, while Noah was building the
ark, but only him , his wife, 3 sons and their wives entered the ark.

(1 Peter 3 v 20)

The flood

It rained for 40 days & nights
The Ark rested 5 months after the flood, for many days on Mount
Ararat (MD Armenia, East Turkey)
In the 10th month one could see the top of the mountains
1st day of the 1st year (In the year of Noah turning 601), the land
was drying
and they came out of the Ark in the 2nd month. (Genesis 7,8)

God's Rainbow

Noah built an altar and brought an offering, a pleasant aroma to God.

God promised, established a covenant that He will never again send a
flood that would destroy the entire earth,
and as the sign:

"I put My rainbow in the clouds,
it shall be a sign for the covenant between Myself & the earth."
(Gen 9 v 11-17)

God also, after the flood, extended for people to eat not only plants &
fruits, but also animals.

God said :

"Every moving living thing shall be food for you.
I give you everything as I had given you the green plants &
vegetables,
but you shall not eat meat (flesh) along with its life; its blood. "

Because life is in its blood (flesh).
(Gen 9 v 3&4 ; Leviticus 7 v 26, Acts 15 v 20 & 21 v 25)

7 December

Noah to Abram

Noah lived another 350 years after the flood, so died around age 950 (Gen 9 v 28,29)

Noah had 3 sons: Shem (fame), Ham (warm) & Japhet (expansion)

God blessed Noah and his 3 sons, and said : "Be fruitful and increase…" From them came all the peoples spread across the globe. (Gen 9 v 18)

Shem (Fame) , 2 years after the flood, had a son called:

Arphaxad (released; a healer) who had:

Cainan (possessor, purchaser) had:

Shelah (Quiet, Prayer- Gen 11) had:

Eber (to cross over/ pass through- Gen 11), had:

Peleg (division - Gen 11), had:

Reu (his friend; his shepherd- Gen 11), had:

Serug (branch- Gen 11), had:

Nahor (scorched - Gen 11), had:

Terah (wild goat, old fool), had a son called:

ABRAM (the father is exalted) and he married Sarai (a princess).

Around this time, people built the Tower of Babel, God confused their language and they spread all over the world.

Abram & Sarai

Terah (age 70) had sons Abram, Nahor & Haran (Haran had a son called Lot, but Haran died in Ur of the Chaldeans)

Abram's wife was called Sarai and Nahor's wife was called Milkah.

The Lord said to Abram:

" Get out of your country and away from your father's house, to a land that I will show you.

I will make you a very big nation and I will bless you and make your name great;

And you will be a blessing.

I will bless those who bless you and curse those who curse you. In you, all the families of the earth will be blessed. (Gen 12 v 1-9)

So Abram came to Canaan (Shechem ~ Samaria initially)
(Gen 12 v 5,6)
The Lord said to him there :
"I will give this land to your descendants."
(Gen 12 v 7)

Abram built an altar for the Lord

He pitched his initial tent between Beth-EL (The House of God) and Ai.
(Gen 13 v 3,4)
And then moved South towards the Negev.(Gen 12)

8 December

Abram and his nephew Lot

Both had a lot of cattle, so Abram, being very humble, offered for Lot to choose an area first;

so Lot chose what 'seemed the best in his eyes' ,
well watered and looked like the garden… (Gen 13 v 1-14)

Later on this area turned out to be exceedingly wicked & sinful against the Lord
- Sodom & Gomorrah and so it was completely destroyed by God.

God's promise & reassurance to Abram

Then the Lord said to Abram:

"Look North, South, East & West (in all directions),
 I will give you all this land,
 and
 your descendants will be innumerable.

Get up and walk through this land, as I give it to you."

So Abram moved his tent to Hebron.
(Hence called the Hebrew people)
(Gen 13 v 14- 18)

Soon after this, Melchizedek, the High priest of God met and blessed Abram, who gave him 1/10 of all his possessions. (Gen 14 v 18-20)

After these things, the word of the Lord came to Abram in a vision:

"Don't be scared Abram, I am your shield, your very great reward.

One from your own body will be your heir.

Look towards Heaven and the stars,
if you can count them, so (many) shall your descendants be."

Abram believed God, and it was accounted to him as righteousness.
(Gen 15 v 1-6)

God also showed him:

That his descendants would be foreigners in a land not their own (Egypt) for 400+ years, but would return to the Promised land (Canaan).
(Gen 15 v 13-21)

Abram to Abraham ~ God's Covenant ~

Sarai to Sarah

When **Abram was 99** years old (And Sarai 90), the Lord appeared to him and said:

" I am almighty God, walk before me, blamelessly.
I will make My Covenant between Me and you,I will multiply you exceedingly.

Abram fell on his face (Bowed down out of respect).

You will be a father of many nations, and your name will no longer be Abram, but from now on ABRAHAM.
And I will give the land of Canaan to you and your descendants forever.
Every male child shall be circumcised at 8 days old. (as a sign of the Covenant between me and you & your descendants)

Sarai (your wife) will now be called Sarah-
I will bless her and give you a son . She will be a mother of nations, kings & people will come (descend) from her.

So,

God made a Covenant with them to be their God
and to bless them to be the father & mother of many nations;

and God changed their names to:

ABRAHAM (Father of many nations) & SARAH (Mother of nations):

By faith Abraham followed God and by faith he lived in a foreign land, because of God's promise to him.

He waited for the city whose Builder and Maker is God (Heaven).
(Hebrews 11 v 8-11)

Sarah

By faith received the 'strength' to conceive in her old age.
Because she trusted God who had promised this, to be faithful.
(Hebrews 11 v 11)

A son was promised to Abraham & Sarah in old age.

The promise of Isaac:

"Is anything impossible for the Lord?
At this time next year I will come back and you will have a son."

And so Sarah and Abraham did. (Gen 18 v 14; Genesis 18, 21)

14 Generations from Abraham to David

9 December

Isaac

- Isaac's name means: 'He will laugh"- because Sarah, his mother, had initially laughed in unbelief at God's promise. (Gen 21)
- Abraham circumcised Isaac at 8 days old as God had commanded him. (Gen 21 v 1-7)
- God tested Abraham re his only son (Gen 22)
- Sarah was 127 years old and then died in Hebron, in Canaan
  (Gen 23 v 1,2)

- Finding a wife for Isaac:
  Abraham said: "Go to my country & my people and find a wife for my son from my own people." (Gen 24 v 4)
- Married Rebekah (Means: joined together, tie, bind) (Gen. 24)
  Rebekah was the Granddaughter of Nahor & Milkah
  (Gen 24 v 24)
- Isaac was comforted after his mother Sarah's death, by his wife; marriage. (Gen 24 v 67)

Isaac & Rebekah (Initial life in Canaan)

- God had reassured Isaac that He would be with him as He was with his father Abraham. (Gen 26 v 23-25)

    Some of the herdsmen in Canaan kept challenging Isaac's herdsmen and he had to move away a few times.
    At Beersheba God said:

    "I am the God of your father Abraham, do not fear, because I am with you. I will bless you." (Gen 26 v 24)

- Isaac & Rebecah had twins: Esau & Jacob:

Esau (hairy, rough)- sold his first-born birth right to his brother Jacob for some lentil soup.

JACOB (Means 'To follow' & 'God protects')

10 December

JACOB

After some time, Isaac sent out Jacob; to find and marry a woman from his mother's people (Esau had married Canaanite wives.)
(Gen 28 v 1-5)

- In Beth-EL:

  Jacob dreamed about a ladder with angels from & to Heaven. The Lord stood above it all and said to Jacob:

  "I am with you and will keep you wherever you go
   and will bring you back to Canaan."

  (Beth means 'house' and El means God ~ So Beth-El means : The House of God. (Gen 28 v 10-22)

- Worked for 7 years for Laban to marry Rachel, but was given Leah.
- Afterwards he was also given Rachel, but had to work another 7 years.
- The Lord was with Jacob and blessed him.
  They all eventually moved away from Laban.

- On his way back to his own family,

God changed Jacob's name to 'Israel' in Peniel.
                (Gen 32, v 30,31; 35 v 10)

- He had 2 wives & 12 sons ~ who represented the 12 tribes of Israel, and 1 daughter.

Leah

(Means Delicate)

Jacob & Leah had:

Reuben, Simeon, Levi, Judah, Issachar, Zebulun, Dinah (sister);
Gad and Asher by Zilpah

Rachel

(means Female)

Jacob & Rachel had:

Joseph & Benjamin;
Dan and Naphtali by Bilhah

Joseph

- God spoke to him through dreams -
  this made his brothers very jealous & angry,
- They threw him in a pit, wanting to kill him.
  But he ended up being sold by his jealous brothers to slavery in Egypt.

- God was with Joseph and he eventually became second in charge in Egypt (except for Pharoah)
  (After false accusations & imprisonment)

- God enabled Joseph to explain the Pharaohs' dreams
- During the famine in Canaan and more , Joseph provided for his family in Egypt:

"To save lives, God has sent me ahead of you".

Joseph had found the grace to forgive his siblings and trust God's plan.
(Gen 37 - 45)

Judah

- Means 'thanksgiving & praise' - half brother of Joseph , Jacob was both's father.
- Had twin sons (born in Canaan)
  By a woman who had disguised herself as a prostitute (but he found out later, it was his daughter-in-law, who had been angry that his other son was not given to her as husband, when hers had died)

PEREZ (burst forth he was called; to be born first, as he had a twin brother called Zerah too). As an adult, Perez (still in Canaan) had:

HEZRON (stronghold, walled enclosure) (Ruth 4 v 18)

- Born in Canaan ,
- Migrated to Egypt as a child with Judah his Grandfather, and Jacob his Great grandfather, and his uncles, aunt and family
- (11 tribes of Israel, the 12th one Joseph was already there)

Above 2 were born in Canaan, moved with Jacob, and Judah, and the other 10 brothers and the whole family (of 70) to Egypt.
(Gen 46 v 12)

Judah

Moved to Egypt with his brothers (on inviting from Joseph, who was already established there);
 And with his father Jacob & mother Leah and all the children & grandchildren (total of 70).
(Rachel had died giving birth to Benjamin in Canaan).

11 December

Life in Egypt: Provision

70 Souls (people) moved from their initial life in Canaan to Egypt:

Jacob & his family moved during the great famine that was in all of Canaan,
from near Hebron, Mamre, where they had been living.

The Names of all who moved to Egypt is documented in:
GENESIS 46 v 8-27 & EXODUS 1 v 1-5

Jacob (now older) - At Beersheba, on the edge of Canaan, stopped and offered sacrifices to God:

God assured Jacob that He was with him and would bless his family into a big nation. (Gen 46 v 1)

God provided well through Joseph's position in Egypt for all his family.

Joseph had 2 children born to him, from his Egyptian wife:
Manasseh & Ephraim.

Jacob regarded them as his own 2 sons and blessed them at his death bed, some years later, at a good age of 147 years, in Egypt.*

However, Jacob was buried in Canaan-
His sons took his body there and he was buried in the cave which Abraham had bought when Sarah had died, alongside them and also:
Isaac & Rebekah,
and his wife Leah, in Mamre, Hebron. (Gen 49 v 29-33)

Modern day Hebron still exists, a city in the West bank.

Born in Egypt:

Hezron (who had moved as a child from Canaan to Egypt) & his wife had a son called:

RAM (Greek for Highlands ~ Aram or Arni is the Hebrew equivalent)
     (1 Chron 2 v 25) ; later on had a son called:

Amminadab (my people are noble)
Daughter Elisheba was married to Aaron (Exodus 6 v 23 - 26)
Amminadab's son was:

Nashon (foundation, pillar, leader)
Leader of the Judah tribe (Numbers 1,2)

Prophecy & Promise

* When Jacob was dying:
He blessed all his children and to Judah he spoke these prophetic words

"The Sceptre shall not depart from Judah ,
until Shiloh (means The Messiah) comes. "   (More in Gen 49 v 10-12)

Joseph eventually grew old too and died at age 110 years,
with the promise that God will take them out of Egypt to the Promised land, and that they should take his bones with them.
(which they did when the time came). (Gen 50 v 22-26)

Slavery

After some time, a new Pharaoh took over as ruler of Egypt;
He did not know about Joseph and treated the Israelites very harshly.

He also instructed the cruel killing of all their baby boys;

But

A baby boy was hidden and saved by his mother (and sister) -
his name was Moses.

Moses

- Adopted by the Egyptian princess and brought up in their Royal
  Palace.

- Later on God called Moses to lead the Israelites out of Egypt to
  the promised land.*

  God appeared to Moses in a 'burning bush'. (See Exodus 3)

(* With the help of his brother Aaron.
And they had a sister Miriam, who was a prophetess .)

- God usually speaks to His prophets through dreams & visions,
  But God spoke to Moses face to face and called him 'His friend.'
                                                      (Exod 33 v 11)
                                                   (Numbers 12 v 6-8)

Note:

Moses was not perfect at all;
40 years earlier, he had killed an Egyptian abuser, then had fled;
but some years later, God had called him back for this huge task.
                                                    (Exodus 1 - 10)
God can & wants to forgive us any wrongs;
and give us a wholesome purpose for our lives.

Exodus-escape

God sent 10 plagues to get the Pharaoh to let His people go.

The 10 plagues that came on Egypt:

1. *The Nile river (all the water) turned into blood.*
2. *Frogs*
3. *Lice*
4. *Flies*
5. *A pestilence (disease) that killed the Egyptian livestock*
6. *Boils*
7. *Hail*
8. *Locusts*
9. *Darkness*

The Lord God said to Moses & Aaron:
(Exodus 11 v 1)

"I will send 1 more plague on Pharaoh and on Egypt;
 after this he will let you go."

"I will execute judgement against all the gods of Egypt."

10: The last plague:

Death of all first born males as well as the firstborn of the livestock.
(Exodus 11 v 6-8; 12 v 12)

"But against all the Israelites, whether man or animal, not even a dog will growl or snap.

So that you will know that the Lord makes a distinction between Egypt and Israel."

The Lord (Yahweh) also said to them:

This month is to be the beginning of the year for you;
It is the first month of your (calendar) year.

- Each family should prepare an unblemished 1 year old

  lamb

  to eat it, roasted with unleavened bread & bitter herbs.

- They must take some of the blood,
  and put it on the 2 doorposts & lintel of the houses
  (in which they are).

You must eat it like this:

Dressed for travel, sandals on your feet, staff in the hand.
You must eat it in a hurry.

It is the Lord's Pass Over.

I will pass through the land of Egypt on this night
and strike every first born male.

I am the Lord

I will execute judgement against all the gods of Egypt.

The blood on the houses where you are staying will be the
distinguishing mark for you-

When I see the blood , I will pass over you.

There will be no plague destroying you, when I strike the land of Egypt.
(Gen 12 v 1-27)

The Israelites did this, just as the Lord had commanded.
(Exodus 12 v 28)

At midnight the Lord struck Egypt and all happened as above.
(Exodus 12 v 29-36)

And that night (early hours of the morning) the Pharaoh let the Israelites leave Egypt.

The Israelites had been living in Egypt for about 430 years.
600 000 men & their families left that night (Exodus 12 v 37)
A mixed crowd also left with them.
And large droves of livestock & other possessions.

God held a vigil for His people's safe exit that night.
God went ahead of them in a pillar of cloud in the day,
and a pillar of fire at night. (Exodus 13 v 21,22)

After a short while, the Pharaoh changed his mind
and pursued them with his forces. (Exodus 14 v 13,14)

Moses said to the people:

" Don't be scared:

Stand still and see the salvation that the Lord
(The Great I AM; Yahweh) will accomplish for you today-

 Because the Egyptians you see today,
you will never see again." (Exodus 14 v 13)

The Angel of God came and stood behind the Israelites, and
The cloud (The Lord) moved from the front to the back,
between them and their persecutors.

God opened the Red sea (still active today) ,miraculously so for them
and they went through on dry land:

The enemy pursuing them, all drowned. (Exodus 14 v 21-31)

12 December

In the wilderness

- God's presence was with His people day and night
  (the pillar cloud and fire)
- He provided bread (called Manna) that rained from Heaven
  And quail (meat) to eat,
  And enough water -Miraculously from a rock and from springs
  Even their clothes did not wear out

- Aaron made them a sinful idol (golden calf) when they had
  become impatient

- On Mount Sinai- God gave the 10 commandments (via Moses)
- God instructed Moses to construct a 'Meeting tent', where He
  met with Moses in a 'cloud' in the most Holy area.
  It was separated with a curtain (veil) from the Holy area
  (The Ark of the Old Covenant was kept here - this contained the
  2 stone 'tablets' with the law written on it by God & Aaron's staff).

The 10 commandments

1. You must not have other gods
2. You must not have any idols
3. Don't speak the Name of the Lord God in vain, or take an oath in His Name in vain.
4. Sabbath day- remember it and keep it holy
   (A separate day - for rest and fellowship with Believers; God also rested)
5. Honour parents
6. Don't murder
7. Don't commit adultery
8. Don't steal
9. Don't give false witness against your neighbour
10. Don't covet your neighbours house, wife or possessions

- Heading for the Promised Land (Canaan-as ordained by God)-

  Moses sent out 12 spies, they came back with good reports about the Promised Land, but

  Only JOSHUA & Caleb were positive that they could beat the 'Giants' there.

- Moses knew the Lord God face to face.
  And God had done many miracles through him.(Deut 34 v 1-10)

Moses had prophesied (About the Messiah):

"Yahweh your God will raise up a Prophet for you ,
from your own people, to Him you will listen." (Deut 18 v 15)

<u>Before Moses parted from this life on earth, he spoke these words:</u>

"Look, I set before you today life & prosperity or death & destruction.

Love the Lord and walk in obedience to Him;
keep His commands , decrees & laws and then you will live and increase and the Lord your God will bless you.

But if your hearts turn away and you are disobedient;
and if you are drawn away & bow down to other gods and worship them; I declare to you that you will be destroyed.

I set before you Life and death; Blessing or curse

Now choose life, that you & your children may live;

And that you may love the Lord your God, listen to His voice and hold
fast to Him.
For the Lord (God) is your life
and will give you many years in the land... "
(Deuteronomy 30)

"This commandment is not too difficult for you or beyond your
reach;
It is in your mouth and in your heart, that you can obey it."
(Deut. 30 v 11-14)

Moses was 120 years old when he died, yet his eyes were not weak nor
had his strength gone.
(Likely because He spent so much one to one time with God).

After Moses & Aaron had died;God called Joshua to lead further…
(Exodus, Leviticus, Numbers, Deuteronomy, Joshua)

Nashon
Born in Egypt,
Leader of the Judah tribe in the wilderness
(Sister Elisheba was married to Aaron as mentioned before)
Means: foundation, pillar (Numbers 1, 2)

Joshua- new leader

Joshua (son of Nun) was filled with the Holy Spirit,
because Moses had Divinely laid hands on him, (Deut 34 v 9)

Appointed by God to take over from Moses;
To lead the people from the wilderness into the Promised Land.

The Lord God said to Joshua:

"Nobody will be able to stand against you all the days of your life.
I will be with you, just as I was with Moses.
I will not leave you nor forsake you.

Be strong and courageous, as you will lead these people to inherit the land that I had promised to give them.

Be strong and very courageous to do all the laws I had commanded you to, by Moses.

Because then you will prosper in what you do.

Be strong and of good courage;

Don't be afraid or dismayed for Yahweh your God is with you wherever you go."

(Joshua 1 v 5-9)

Spying on Jericho

Joshua, the new leader, sent out 2 spies to Canaan…(Joshua 2 v 1-22)

Rahab (a prostitute) hid the spies; she said:

" I know that Yahweh has given you this land;

- We are terrified of you and all the inhabitants of our land (Jericho & Canaan) are faint hearted because of you.
- We have heard how Yahweh had dried up the water of the Red sea for you to walk through.
- And how you defeated the 2 Amorite kings …

As soon as we heard about these things 'our hearts melted & all our courage left us', because,

Yahweh your God: He is God in Heaven above and on earth below."

So she hid the 2 spies…. even told the local soldiers they had gone in a different direction, to help and save the people of God.
Rahab had chosen to leave behind her old life and all that entailed, to follow the Living God.
(She is also commended for her faith, in Hebrews 11).

She asked them to promise to save her and her family,
when they would attack Jericho. (Which they did).

The spies reported back to Joshua:

" All the people are melting in fear, because of us."
(Joshua 2 v 24)

13 December

Crossing the Jordan river

- The people purified themselves,
- The priests entered the water first, with the Ark of the Covenant (Presenting God's presence) at the front:
- God miraculously again opened up a pathway for all His people to walk through safely. (Joshua 3)

Nashon & his wife had a son:

Salmon (aka Sala in Hebrew)

- Means: mission, sending, stretching out– for the future (he 'stretched out, reached out' to Canaan…)
- Born in the wilderness
- Entered the Promised land (Canaan)

In Canaan:

Renewal of OT Covenant & First Passover

(Joshua 1-4)

Shortly after setting up camp in Gilgal (after crossing the Jordan into the Promised land), God commanded them to:

- Circumcise all the men (born in the wilderness) according to the (Old) testament Covenant with God.

- Soon after this, they took their First Passover in Canaan their Promised Land.

  Also the 'manna' (bread from heaven) stopped and they ate 'of the fruit of the land of Canaan' that year and day.

- Gilgal means 'to roll'- God said to His people:
  " Today I have rolled away the reproach from Egypt."

  Ancient day: East of Jericho; Modern day area : East of the Jordan river

Battle of Jericho

Even though the People of God had entered the Promised Land,
They had several battles to fight.

And Jericho was their first, and certainly a big one. But for God!
Joshua was still the leader of God's people.
(Joshua 5 v 13-15)

The Commander of the Lord's armies met Joshua outside Jericho and
there the Lord said to Joshua:
"Look; See (!):
I have delivered Jericho, its king and fighting men into your hands."

"Do this: March around the city and…"
Read the full amazing story of miraculous victory in Joshua 5 & 6.

Joshua led them to several victories as long as they followed God and His ways. On one occasion they lost to the small city of Ai, due to 'sin in the camp.'

Joshua , shortly before his death at age 110 years, said to the people:

"Choose you this day whom you will serve, (the gods of this or that…)
but for me & my family- we will serve the Lord God (Yahweh)."

Salmon & Rahab

Salmon married Rahab in Canaan.

*She was the previously mentioned prostitute woman in Jericho,
but because she had acknowledged God to be the true God;
and helped save His people (by hiding the 2 spies on her roof top);*

*As promised, she and her family were saved during the battle of Jericho.
(Joshua 2 & Hebrew 11, Matthew 1 v 5)*

Salmon & Rahab had a son called BOAZ.

14 December

Boaz & Ruth

They lived in the time of the Judges- The leaders of God's people, after Joshua had died.
Judges 1 - 21 (Eg Gideon, Samson, Deborah...) about 1200 BC.

BOAZ

Means: strength, swiftness. North pillar
A wealthy landowner in Bethlehem
An honourable & generous man
Kind to the poor & foreigners
Had integrity- followed the law
A kinsman-redeemer

RUTH

Means: compassionate; friend
Originally a Moabite woman who followed Naomi (her mother-in-law)
and Naomi's GOD (Yahweh).
Earlier on Naomi had moved with her husband to Moab during a famine
in Canaan, but lost her husband & sons there & moved back to Canaan.

Ruth said to Naomi:

"I will go where you go, I will lodge where you do,
Your people will be my people, and your God, my God
and where you die, I will too." (Ruth 1-4)

BOAZ & RUTH married and had a son:

OBED (Servant of God) .

Obed to David

Obed & his wife had a son called:

JESSE
Means: The Lord exists
A farmer & sheep breeder in Bethlehem
Had 8 sons & 2 daughters (1 Samuel 16,17)
Lived In the time of God's prophet Samuel

Jesse's youngest son was called:

DAVID (Means: Beloved, Beloved one, Friend)

Shepherd boy to king David

In the time when David was a young boy, The Israelites asked God for a 'human king'.
God gave them Saul as their first king; the prophet Samuel anointed him.
More details in the books of 1,2 Samuel; 1,2 Kings & 1,2 Chronicles

- Shepherd boy- learned with God's help to fend off the lion & bear
  (1 Sam 17 v 34-36)
- Skilled with a sling & stone
- Played the harp
- Anointed by the prophet Samuel to become king
  (when king Saul had turned away from God) (1 Sam 16)

- Beat the Giant Goliath (1 Sam 17)

  David said to the Philisistine:

  "You come to me with a sword & with a spear & with a javelin,

  But I come to you in the Name of Yahweh, the God of armies (hosts);
  the God of the armies of Israel-
  whom you have taunted (defied, insulted, reproached).

- Military leader under king Saul
- People favoured him
  ("Saul conquered thousands, but David conquered 10 1000's")
- David faced many challenges:
  - King Saul wanted to kill him because of jealousy, so he persistently pursued him (1 Sam 18,19)
  - His son (Absalom) even wanted to kill him at some point, to take the kingdom off him (2 Sam 15-18)
- God provided a loyal trustworthy , helpful friend in Jonathan (king Saul's son) (1 Sam 20)

- David wrote 73 of the 150 Psalms, e.g.

Psalm 23: The Lord is my Shepherd.

Psalm 16:
" I see the Lord (Yahweh) continually before me,
  Because He is at my right hand, I will not be moved or shaken."
  (Ps 16 v 8)
- Prophesied about the coming of the Messiah: Ps 2,16,22,110,118

- He loved the Lord & He loved to be in the house of the Lord.
  (The Tabernacle in Gibeon, later Jerusalem).
- He sought the Lord's guidance in his decisions (most of them…)
- He regularly strengthened himself in the Lord
- He spoke to; poured out his heart to God frequently
- God loved David- a man after God's own heart. (1 Sam 13 v 14)

David became king:
Firstly of the Kingdom of Judah & then all Israel
(after Saul's death)
- David captured Jerusalem city and made it the political & spiritual capital.
- Brought the Ark of the Covenant to Jerusalem .
- Established the Kingdom of Israel
- Defeated all their enemies at the time

15 December

David's fall, repentance & restoration

David had an adulterous relationship with a married woman
(Bathsheba) and also arranged for her husband to be at the front line of
the war, and so he was killed.

God sent His prophet Nathan to address this and seriously reprimand
David about it.

David then wrote Psalm 51

> " <u>I have sinned against You God...</u>
>
> <u>Create in me a pure heart oh God..."</u>

Their first child became ill and died, but God, in His great mercy,
forgave David &Bathsheba and gave them 2 more sons.

God's mercy and David & Bathsheba's sons:

Solomon & Nathan

Joseph- Father on earth of the Messiah,
        Family line came from King Solomon

Mary- Mother of the Messiah
        Family line came from Nathan

God's immense mercy and grace was shown to David & Bathsheba;

And God continues to offer the same mercy and forgiveness today;
to anyone who says sorry and starts again.

Thankfully we don't have to do this in our own power or strength…
but through Christ and the Holy Spirit.
(More on this at the end of this book).

David wanted to build a house (Temple for God) in Jerusalem,
because the meeting place with God had been in a tent (tabernacle) -in
the Most Holy section, separated by a curtain; whilst in the wilderness.

Now in the Promised land, the Ark of the Covenant. (Presenting God's
Presence) had nowhere properly to be kept.

God promised David that his son Solomon would build the Temple &
God promised that he would be with Solomon always,
Even if he was to go astray; the wrong way-
for the sake of David and for the sake of His Messiah to come….

"He (Solomon) shall build a house for My Name
 and I will establish the throne of his kingdom forever."
(2 Samuel 7 v 16)

DAVID made preparations for his son Solomon to build a house
(Temple) for God, to replace the Tent (Tabernacle) of meeting.

The Ark of the Covenant would be placed in the Holiest area of the
Temple, where the High priest used to meet with God once a year for the
atonement of people's sins.

('Normal Priests' also did bring daily sin offerings , burnt offerings & burn incense in the Holy
place of the Tent (or Temple), and they lit the 7 candles with 'Holy olive oil that were burning
24/7. Olive oil represents the Holy Spirit of God).

The books of: Kings & Chronicles explain all the happenings relating to all the Kings of Israel
as a combined Kingdom.
Elijah & Elisha were 2 significant prophets whom God spoke through during the above time.

There was 14 generations from King David to Exile in BABYLON

16 December

Genealogy of Joseph (Earthly father to the Messiah) , from Solomon onwards

King SOLOMON (means PEACE)

The Good:

- Asked God for wisdom,
  but God also blessed him with wealth & a long life
- Built God's temple (house) in Jerusalem. (1 Kings 5-8)
- Was very wise, (and was famous & wealthy) (1 Kings 9,10)
- Wrote Proverbs, Ecclesiastes, Song of Songs & some Psalms
  (e.g. Ps 72)
- Reigned for 40 years over Israel

The Bad:

- He made compromises with his many foreign wives and their
  gods & idols, dishonouring the Living God. (1 Kings 11)
- Started to impose too harsh taxes and labour towards the end of
  his reign.

(More on him in: 2 Samuel 12 v 24,25; 1 Kings 1,2,3; 1 Chron 28, 29)

After Solomon's death, his son took over:

King Rehoboam.

King REHOBOAM (Enlarged Nation)

- Ruled in Jerusalem after his father Solomon's death (930 BC)
- Due to making the burden (heavy taxes & forced labour) on his people too harsh, the Kingdom of Israel split into two:

Jeroboam, an official of King Solomon had led the 10 Northern tribes to revolt- and this was now called Samaria/Ephraim- Ref. 1 Kings 12)

The Southern Kingdom, called Judah (& Benjamin)
& The Northern Kingdom, called Israel (10 tribes)

The N Kingdom of Israel and S Kingdom of Judah (combined with Benjamin) from whom the Messiah would come...Prophets during these times were Isaiah, Jeremiah and more.

- He did not follow the Lord, but did repent in the end.
- There was war between him (As king of Judah) and the king of Israel during his entire reign.

The N Kingdom (of Israel) fell into exile in Assyria about 200 years later. (2 Kings 17 v 6)

The Southern Kingdom, called Judah, continued for 136 more years, before going into exile to Babylon.

For the purpose of this book, from this point on, we shall only be following the Kings of Judah (after the Kingdom of Israel was divided as explained above), because the Messiah came from Judah's family line:

The Sceptre will not depart from Judah, until Shiloh comes
(The Messiah) (Gen 49 v 10)
God promise to King David:

"I will establish the throne of his (Solomon's) kingdom forever...
Your throne will be established forever..." (2 Samuel 7 v 12,13,16)

Rehoboam's son was called Abijah.

King ABIJAH (My Father is Yahweh)
Started with God (2 Chron 14 v 2b - 19)
Then he did evil (1 Kings 15 v 3-5)
But God saved them for King David's sake, who did most things right in
God's eyes. His son:

King ASA (ASAPH) (Gatherer)
He did all that was right in God's eyes & destroyed the idols
(2 Chronicles 14 v 1-5). His son:

King JEHOSHAPHAT (Yahweh has judged)
Followed the Lord like his father ASA,
But, did not destroy the high places (2 Chron 20 v 31-33). His son:

King JEHORAM (Yahweh is exalted)
He was an evil king (2 Chron 21). His son:

*(Kings Ahasiah, Joash (2 Kings 13) & Amaziah (2 Kings 14), although documented in the
Old Testament, are not mentioned by Matthew's Genealogy of the Messiah,
because of their wickedness and connection with evil Ahab & Jezebel's daughter)*

King Uzzia (Name means: The Lord is my strength) (aka Azariah)
792- 740 BC (Prophets: Isaiah , Amos, Hosea, Jonah, Micah)
Strong & Prosperous king, reigned 52 years *(2 Chron 22, 26 v 1)*
Initially served God well, but allowed pride into his life, and died with
leprosy. *(2 Chron 26),* His son:

King JOTHAM (God is perfect):
750-735 BC ; Prophet Micah (Hosea spoke to the Northern Kingdom of Israel)
A Godly king (2 Chron 27)

Micah prophesied in this time:

"But you Bethlehem (Ephrathat),
though you are small (amongst the Judah clans)-
Out of you will come for Me, One who will be ruler ;
whose origins are from old, from ancient times." (Micah 5 v 2)

King AHAZ (The Lord holds) was the son of King Jotham:
735-715 BC (Prophets Micah, Isaiah)
Started evil, But repented and was forgiven. (2 Kings 16)

In this time GOD spoke promises through the prophet Isaiah:

(Isaiah was God's prophet during the time of King Uzziah, Jotham, Ahaz & Hezekiah)

"The virgin will conceive and bear a son, and His name will be:
Immanuel- God is with us."

"The people will see a Great light, those walking in darkness will see a
Glorious light."

"Wonderful counsellor, Mighty God,Father of the Everlasting,Prince of
Peace." (YLT)

God would send Immanuel, His Messiah (Saviour), His Son.
(Isaiah 7 v 10-16, 9 v 1-7)

King Ahaz' son was called Hezekiah:

King HEZEKIAH (God Strengthens)

715-686 BC (Prophets Micah & Isaiah's later prophecies)

- A very Godly king (2 Kings 18)
- Reinstated the Passover celebration, amongst other Godly things.
- God spoke via Isaiah to him.

He got ill to the point of dying and he cried to the Lord God and prayed:

> God answered:
> "I have heard your prayers and seen your tears…I have answered your prayers"
>
> .
>
> He was healed. (2 Kings 20 v 5)

After his recovery, he & his wife had a son called:

Manasseh (which means: God has made me forget).

(Forget his illness & troubles).

King Manasseh
697-642 BC
Nahum was a prophet during his reign, judgement on Assyria (after Jonah's time)
Sadly, was one of the most idolatrous kings of Judah
Started evil; ended up in a dungeon;
Repented and was forgiven, had a son called:

King AMON (Faithful)
642-640 BC
King at 22, sadly also served idols, only ruled 2 years
Did not humble himself before God,
was assassinated by his servants; his son:

King JOSIAH (God supports and heals)
640-609 BC,
Prophet Jeremiah from 627BC ;Habakkuk was also a prophet during this time
(from 612-589 BC) and Zephaniah started to prophesy (640-609BC)

King Josiah walked in God's ways like never before and never after him.

JEHOAHAZ very short reign, so not even included ;
JEHIOAKIM 609-598BC also not mentioned in the family line

King Josiah had a son called:

King JECONIAH (aka as Jehoiachin)

and then the exile to Babylon took place. *598-597BC*

JEREMIAH was a prophet during this time up to Jeconiah and also during exile for some time
OBADIAH 586 BC around the fall of Jerusalem.

(Zedekiah not in the genealogy as he was not in the bloodline)

597-586 BC ; Prophet Jeremiah & Babylonian exile

17 December

Exile in Babylon 586-538 BC

14 Generations from Exile to the Messiah

The EXILE happened because of the ongoing rebellion against God, and the persistent sinning of Judah.

Note,they were not called kings any longer, as they were living under a foreign king in a foreign country now…King Nebuchadnezzar in Babylon

JECONIAH (YAH ,God, Has established)

He was the very last king of Judah,
and he had brothers at the time of exile
Jeremiah prophesied that his line would be preserved.
(Jer 22 v 30, 33 v 17) ; his son was:

SHEALTIEL (I asked God for this child)
Not mentioned in Matthew, but see OT reference -
PEDIAH (REDEMPTION OF THE LORD) - Biological father of Zerubbabel- 1 Chron 3 v 19

Shealtiel's <u>adopted son</u> was Zerubbabel (born in Babel)

ZERUBBABEL

(Means Conceived & born in Babylonian captivity)
(Matt 1 v 12)

Prophets during the time of exile were:

Jeremiah (God's promise of restoration), Ezekiel & Daniel (in Babylon)

God spoke this message through his prophet*,
while the people were in exile:

"I know the plans I have for you, declares God-
thoughts of peace and not of evil;
to give you a future and a hope
To prosper you and not to harm you." (*Jeremiah 29 v 11)

They were in exile for about 70 years.
After this,
Zerubbabel led the first group of exiled people back to Jerusalem.
538 BC, under the Decree of Cyrus, King of Persia.

Nehemiah:

Cup bearer to the Persian king while in exile.
Governor to oversee the restoration of God's city and Temple.
God brought an *encouraging message via this prophet during the further*
returns of exiled people at the time:

"Start with the work, don't disregard the day of small beginnings."

Nehemiah helped to oversee the work.
Rebuilding the wall of Jerusalem & temple of God- which the
Babylonians had destroyed.

Ezra:

(A priest & Scribe):
Brought the scriptures & reminded (taught) people of the Ways of the
Lord.Those who had returned from exile.

Post-exile

After 538 BC

Zerubbabel was the governor alongside Joshua the high priest.

Prophets:
Haggai: 520 BC, Encouraged rebuilding of the temple
Zehariah:
520-518BC,Visions & Messianic promises & hope during the rebuilding

Malachi: 450-430 BC, Final Old testament prophet
Covenant faithfulness of the future Messiah & 'Elijah' (pointing to John the baptist, to precede this)

After the last OT prophet Malachi spoke,
there was a period of 400 years of 'silence' (4 to 5 generations...)

Zerubbabel's son was:

ABIHUD (The Divine Father is Glory) who was the father of:

ELIAKIM (God will establish, God rises),
but he was called JEHOIAKIM by Pharaoh Necho II, his son was:

AZOR (Helper) who had:

ZADOK (Just ; Righteous) who had:

ACHIM (Preparing) who had:

ELIUD (God's grandeur, God is my praise) who had:

ELEAZAR (God has helped) who had:

MATTHAN (Giving) who had:

JACOB (Follow, heal, My God protects) whose son was: Joseph…

JOSEPH (Means: God will add)

Joseph would be Mary's husband, of whom the Messiah would be born.

Summary:
(Matthew 1 v 1 - 17)

14 generations from Abraham to David

14 generations from David to the Exile in Babylon

14 generations from the Exile in Babylon to the return and the Birth of the Messiah.

18 December

Genealogy of Mary (mother of the Messiah)

from Nathan onwards

(Luke 3 v 23b to 38)

Brother of Solomon, Also a son of King David & Bathsheba was:

NATHAN (God gave; Gift of God), who became the father of

MELEA (Completeness;fullness) father of

ELIAKIM (GOD will establish) father of

JONAM (GIFT OF GOD) father of

JOSEPH (GOD SHALL ADD) father of

JUDAH (PRAISE) father of

SIMEON (GOD HAS HEARD) father of

LEVI (JOINED) father of

MATTHAT (GIFT OF GOD) father of

JORIM (YAH - God - IS EXALTED) father of

ELIEZER (God is help) father of

JOSHUA (God's deliverance) father of

ER (Awake) father of

ELMODAM (The God of measure; Garment) father of

COSAM (Diving) father of

ADDI (Adorned) father of

MELDI (Melody) father of

NERI (My candle, lamp or light) father of

SALATIEL (Pray to God, Intercessor) father of

ZERUBBABEL (born in Babel exile) , the father of

RHESA (Will; course) father of

JOANAN (God is gracious) father of

JUDAH (Praised) father of

JOSECH (Fame taken away, but Yahweh,God, will add) father of

SEMEIN (Hear distinctly) father of

MATTATHIAS (The gift of God) father of

MAATH (Wiping away) father of

NUGGAI (Reflect light) father of

ESLI (Reserved of God) father of

NAHUM (Comforter) father of

AMOS (Carry -the burden of the rebellious people) father of

MATTATHIAS (Gift of God) father of

JOSEPH (God shall add) father of

JANNAI (God answers) father of

MELCHI (My King, My Counsel) father of

LEVI (Joined) father of

MATTHAT (Gift of God) father of

HELI (ASCENDING/ SUN)

And Heli was the father of:

MARY

Means: Beloved, A drop of the sea (ocean)

The Mother of the Messiah (Saviour) sent by God

19 December

The Witness to The Light

There (would) appear a man, having been sent from God, his name: John.

He (would) come as a witness, that he could testify about the Light, that everyone may believe through him.

He was not the Light, but he would witness about the Light.

The true Light, who enlightens every person, was coming into the world.

(John 1 v 6-9)

The angel Gabriel appears to Zechariah

A Message from God

During the time (reign) of king Herod of Judea, there was a priest called Zechariah (of Abijah's division) and his wife was a descendant of Aaron's daughters, and her name was Elizabeth.

Now they both were righteous in God's sight, walking (living) blamelessly in all the commandments and requirements of the Lord.
And they had no children, as Elizabeth was infertile (barren), and they were both 'advanced in years.

Now it happened, while fulfilling (doing) his priestly duties (service), in the appointed order of his division before God,
According to the custom of the priesthood, it fell on him by lot, to burn incense, when he had entered the temple of the Lord (God).

And all the many people were praying outside, at the time (hour) of the incense.

Then an angel of the Lord (God) appeared to him, standing at the right (side) of the altar of incense.

And having seen him, Zechariah was perplexed (troubled) and he became scared ('fear fell on him'.)

Then the angel said to him:

"Do not be afraid, Zechariah, because your prayer has been heard, and your wife will give you a son, and you shall call him 'John'.

And he will give you joy and gladness (happiness), and many (people) will be glad (rejoice) because of his birth.

Because he will be great ('Mega') in the Lord's sight,
And he will not drink wine or strong drinks,
And he will be filled with the Holy Spirit,
even from within his mother's womb.

And he will turn many of the children of Israel to the Lord, their God.

And he will go ahead of Him, in the spirit and power of Elijah, to turn the father's hearts to their children; and the disobedient, to the wisdom of the righteous, to make people prepared and ready for the Lord."

Then Zechariah said to the angel:

"How will I know this? For I am an old man, and my wife has advanced in years?"

Answering him, the angel said:

"I am Gabriel, the one standing in God's presence (before God),
And I was sent to speak to you, and to bring you this good news.

And see, you will be quiet (silent), unable to speak, until the day that
these things will happen, because you did not believe my words
(message), which will be fulfilled in their season. (at the due time)."

And the people (outside) were expecting Zechariah, and they were
wondering why he had been delayed in the temple.

Then when he came out, he was unable to speak to them, and they
knew that he had seen a vision in the temple.
He made signs to them but remained unable to speak. ('mute').

(Luke 1 v 5 - 22)

Elizabeth

It happened when the days of his service (at the temple) were
completed, he went back to his house.

After these days, his wife Elizabeth conceived,
and she hid herself for 5 months,
saying:

"The Lord has done this for me, in the time (days) he looked at me;
(He saw me), to take away my reproach (disgrace) amongst people."

(Luke 1 v 23 -25)

20 December

The angel Gabriel appears to the virgin MARY ~ Message from GOD

Now when Elizabeth was about 6 months pregnant, the angel Gabriel was sent by God, to a city in Galilee, called Nazareth.

To a virgin, engaged to a man, whose name was Joseph, from the house (family) of David, and the virgin's name was Mary.

When he came to her, he said:

"Greetings to you, who are favoured with grace!
The Lord is with you, you are blessed amongst women."

She was perplexed by this statement, and was wondering, what kind of a greeting this is.

So, the angel said to her:

" Don't be scared, Mary, because you have found favour with God.
And behold (see), you will conceive in your womb,
and will give birth to a son, and you shall call him Jesus.

He will be GREAT (Megas),
and will be called the Son of the Most High (God),
And the Lord God will give him the throne of David, His father (forefathers).

And He will reign over Jacob's house forever;
and there will be no end to His Kingdom.

Then Mary said to the angel:

" How will this come about, since I am not in an intimate relationship with a man? "

Answering her, the angel said to her:

'The Holy Spirit will come upon you, and the power of the Most High (God) will overshadow you, therefore also, the Holy (One) being born, will be called, the Son of God.

Look, your relative Elizabeth, she also has conceived a son and that in her old age, and she is in her 6 months of pregnancy already, she who had been called 'barren. (infertile).

Because NOTHING WILL BE IMPOSSIBLE WITH GOD."

Then Mary said:

"Behold the handmaiden of the Lord, may it happen to me, according to your message (Rhema word), and the angel departed from her. "

(Luke 1 v 26 - 38)

21 December

Mary's visit to Elizabeth

Then in those days Mary got up and went to the hill country in a hurry, to a town of Judah.

She entered Zechariah's house and greeted Elizabeth.
And it so happened that, as soon as Elizabeth heard Mary's greeting, the baby inside her womb leapt because of happiness; and Elizabeth was filled with the Holy Spirit.

And she spoke out aloud and said:

"You are blessed amongst women, and blessed is the fruit of your womb.
And how come (I am blessed that) this is happening to me,
That the mother of my Lord should come to me?

Because see:

As soon as my ears heard the voice of your greeting, the baby inside my womb leapt (jumped) because of extreme gladness.

And blessed is the one who has believed that there will be a performance (fulfilment) of the things spoken to her by the Lord. "

Mary praises & thank God

Mary said:

"My soul magnifies the Lord, and my spirit rejoices in God, my Saviour.
Because He has noticed the humiliation of His 'handmaiden',
See from now on, all generations will count me blessed.

Because the Mighty One, has done HUGE (Mega) things for me,
And His Name is Holy.

And He gives mercy to generations and generations of those who revere (fear) Him.

He has displayed strength with His arm.
He has scattered the pride of heart and thoughts.

He has brought down rulers from thrones and has lifted up (exalted) the humble.

The hungry He has filled with good things, and the rich He sent away empty handed.

He has helped Israel His servant, showing (remembering) mercy.
As He spoke to our (fore) fathers, to Abraham and his descendants forever."
(Luke 1 v 39 to 55)

Mary stayed with her (Elizabeth) for about 3 months and then returned to her home. (Luke 1 v 56)

22 December

John the Baptist

(Luke 1 v 57 -79)

Birth

For Elizabeth the time had come to give birth, and she gave birth to a son.
And when her neighbours and relatives heard that,
They magnified (praised) the Lord (God) for His mercy for her and they were glad about her.

Then it so happened on the 8th Day, that they came to circumcise the child, and were going to give him his father's name, Zechariah.

Naming

And his mother answered and said:
"No, he will be called John."

And they said to her: "None of your relatives are called this name?"
Then they made signs to his father, to ask what he would want him to be called. After his father had asked for a writing tablet, he wrote and said:
 "John is his name"; and they all were amazed.

Prophecies concerning him

His mouth was immediately 'opened' then; and his tongue,
and he spoke, blessing God.
Fear came upon all of them; those living around them,
And in all the hill countryside of Judea people talked about all these things.

And all those who heard this, kept it in their hearts, saying:
" What kind of a child is this going to be then ? "

Because the hand of the Lord was with him.

Then Zechariah his father was filled with the Holy Spirit and prophesied:

"Blessed be the Lord God of Israel,
Because He has visited and redeemed His people.

And has raised up a horn of salvation for us,
In the house (family) of David, His servant, as He had spoken
through the mouth of His holy prophets of old.

Salvation from our enemies and from the hand of all those who hate
us. To fulfil mercy to our fathers, and to remember His Holy
covenant.
To grant us the oath that He swore to Abraham, our father.

Having been saved from the hands of our enemies,
To serve Him without fear.
In holiness and righteousness all the days of our lives.

And now you, child, will be called: Prophet of the Most High.
Because you will go ahead of the Lord, to prepare His ways.

To give the knowledge of salvation to His people,
In the forgiveness of their sins.

Through the tender compassion of our God,
In which the SUNRISE from (on) High will visit us.
To shine on those sitting in darkness, and in the shadow of
death.

To direct our feet onto the path of PEACE.

23 December

An angel of God appears to Joseph (Mary's fiancé) in a dream

Now this is how the birth of Jesus Christ happened:

Mary His mother was engaged to Joseph, and before they got together (intimately); It was found that she was pregnant, through the Holy Spirit.

Now Joseph, her husband to be, being righteous and not wanting to expose her publicly, planned to let her go in secret.

Now having pondered on these thoughts of him, Look:

An angel of the Lord appeared to him in a dream, saying:

"Joseph, son of David, do not be afraid to take Mary as your wife,
For what has been conceived in her is Holy, from the Spirit.
(Or 'What has been conceived in her is from the Spirit, Holy').

She will give birth to a Son, and you will call Him JESUS:
Because: HE WILL SAVE HIS PEOPLE FROM THEIR SIN."

This then all happened, that would be fulfilled what had been spoken by the Lord, through the prophet, saying:

"See, the virgin will be pregnant (direct translation: carry in her womb) and will give birth to a Son, and they will call Him: IMMANUEL, which translated, is GOD WITH US."

Then Joseph, woken up from his sleep, he did what the angel of the Lord had commanded him to do, and took Mary as his wife, but he did not 'know her' until she had given birth to a son (whom he would name Jesus). (Matthew 1 v 18 - 24)

24 December

Roman Caesar Augustus' Big Census

(Census = People count)

Then it so happened in those days, that a decree was sent out from Caesar Augustus to register (take a register of) the entire world.

This census (registration) first happened when Quirinius was governing Syria.

And everybody went to be registered, each to their own city.

So, then Joseph also travelled to (went up) from Galilee, (out) from the town Nazareth to the City of David, which is called Bethlehem, because his house(descendants) was of the family of David,

To register with Mary, his espoused (married) wife, she was pregnant (expecting a child).
(Luke 2 v 1 - 30)

25 December

A Baby Boy is born, Shepherds & Angels,

His Name is Jesus

A Baby Boy is born:

Then it happened, while being there, the time to give birth had come.

And Mary gave birth to her Son, the firstborn,

And wrapped him in swaddling cloths,
and laid him in a manger,

because there had been no place for them in the inn. (Luke 2 v 6 & 7)

Shepherds & Angels

And there were shepherds in the same region, they lodged in the fields and were looking after their flock at night.

And an angel of the Lord suddenly stood by them, and the glory of the Lord shone around them, and they were very scared.

Then the angel said to them,
"Do not be afraid, because look, (behold):
I bring good news to you, of great happiness (joy), which will be to all people.

Because a Saviour has been born to (for) you today, who is Christ the Lord, in the city of David.

And this is the sign for you:
You will find a baby wrapped in swaddling cloths and lying in a manger."

Suddenly there came (appeared) with the angel, a multitude of the heavenly hosts, praising God, saying:

"Glory to God in the highest (heaven), and peace on earth amongst people with whom He is pleased."

And it happened when the angels were departing from them into heaven, the shepherds said to one another, let us indeed travel (go) as far as Bethlehem, and let us (go) see this (Rhema) word that has happened, which the Lord has made known (revealed) to us.

And having hurried, they came (arrived) and found both Mary and Joseph, and the baby, lying in the manger.

Now having seen this, they 'broadcasted' (made the news known abroad) about the (rhema) news that were told to them, concerning this CHILD.
And all (those) who heard, were amazed (marvelled) about the things that the shepherds had told them.

But Mary 'treasured up' all these (Rhemata) happenings, thinking about it in her heart.

And the shepherds returned, glorifying and praising God, for everything they had heard and seen, as it had been told to them.

(Luke 2 v 8 - 20)

His Name is : Jesus

When the 8 days were completed, to circumcise Him, they named Him:

Jesus (in Hebrew: Yeshua- The Lord is salvation)

Which he had been called by the angel, before He had been conceived in the womb.

(Luke 2 v 21)

26 December

Dedication of Baby Jesus to God

And when the days of their purification were fulfilled according to the law of Moses, they brought Him to Jerusalem, to present Him to the Lord.

As it is written in the law of the Lord:

Every first born male, will be called (is) holy to the Lord

And to offer a sacrifice, according to what was said in the law of the Lord,
A pair of turtledoves or two young pigeons.

(Luke 2 v 22 - 24)

Simeon:

Receives a Blessing, Gives a blessing & prophecy

And behold (look) there was a man in Jerusalem, whose name was
Simeon.
And this man was righteous and devout;
Waiting for the consolation (comforting) of Israel,
and the Holy Spirit was on (in) him.

And it was divinely revealed to him by the Holy Spirit,
that he would not die ('see death'),
until he saw the Christ (Messiah, Saviour) of the Lord (Yahweh, God).

He came in the Spirit into the temple, at the time when the parents were
bringing the child Jesus (into the temple);
They were doing which are customary by the law for Him

Then he (Simeon) received (took) Jesus into his arms,
blessed God and said:
"Now you can let your servant depart in peace, Lord, according to your
word (rhema). Because my eyes have seen your salvation, which you
have prepared for all people to see:

A LIGHT FOR REVELATION OF THE GENTILES,
AND GLORY OF YOUR PEOPLE ISRAEL."

And his father and his mother were amazed (marvelled) at the things
that had been said about Him.

Then Simeon blessed them, and said to Mary His mother:

"Look this child is appointed for the falling and rising of many (people) in
Israel, and as a sign to be spoken against.
And for you also, a sword will go through your soul,
So that the thoughts of many hearts will be revealed." (Luke 2 v 25 - 35)

Anna the Prophetess

There was a prophetess called Anna -
Daughter of Phanuel of the tribe of Asher.
She was very elderly
She had lived with her husband for 7 years when they got married

Then she had been a widow for about 84 years,
She did not leave the temple,
But served with fasting's and prayers night and day.

And coming up (to them) at that specific time ('hour'),
(she) gave praise to God

And spoke about Him (Jesus) to everyone who had been waiting for the
redemption of Jerusalem. (Luke 2 v 36 - 38)

27 December

The Wise men from the East

After Jesus was born in Bethlehem of Judea, at the time of king Herod, (behold) Wise men from the East arrived in Jerusalem, saying:

"Where is He who has been born (as) King of the Jews?
We saw His Star in the East and have come to worship Him."

When king Herod heard this, He was worried (troubled) and all Jerusalem with him.
When he gathered all the chief priests and the scribes of the people, He enquired of them, where the Christ was to be born.
And they said to him:

"In Bethlehem of Judea, because thus has it been written by the prophet:

'And you Bethlehem, land of Judah,
You are by no means the least of the rulers of Judah,
Because from you will come a leader (one leading),
Who will Shepherd My people, Israel.' "

Then Herod, having called the Wise men in secret,
enquired of them, the exact time that the star had appeared.
After sending them to Bethlehem, he said:

"When you have left (gone), search carefully for the Child.
Then when you have found Him, let me know,
So that I also can come and worship Him."
(However, they were Divinely warned in a dream not to do so, as Herod had intended to kill Jesus, so they did not.)

The Star in the sky

After they had 'heard' the king, they left and LOOK:

The star which they had seen in the East, went ahead of them,
 until it arrived;
It stood over (above) the place where the Child was.

When they saw the star, they were glad (rejoiced) with exceedingly great happiness (joy). (Matthew 2 v 1-12)

The Gift & the Gifts

After they entered the house,
they found the Child and (with) Mary His mother,

And they fell to the ground, and they worshipped Him.

They opened their treasures, and they presented gifts to Him:

- **Gold - a gift fitting for a King**

- **Frankincense** - incense burnt, created a beautiful aroma - associated with Deity

- **Myrrh** - Anointing oil for the big commission, Medicinal properties and for embalming of the body. (Matt 2 v 11 - 12)

Reflection on the Meaning of the Gifts:

GOLD

Jesus left the comfort of God's heavenly Kingdom to come to earth to serve.

FRANKINCENSE

Jesus is Deity, the Son of God, and yet chose to become a human being and live amongst people.
Prayers to God are often referred to as incense. (The Levitical priest in the Old Covenant burnt incense each morning and evening in the Tabernacle in the desert and then in the Temple (King Solomon had built for God) .
Jesus represents our PRIEST and PRAYER to GOD the Father.
In heaven are golden bowls of incense, the prayers of God's children. (Revelation 5 v 8)

MYRRH

For Anointing:

Jesus was anointed by God's Holy Spirit 'ascending on Him immediately after being Baptised as an adult by John the Baptist. (Matthew 3 v 15)
To bring His ministry of new birth and new life - forgiveness, cleansing, healing, happiness, hope, peace …. Eternal redemption and Eternal Life.

For embalming:

For Jesus' eventual death on the Cross, but also- praise God- for His resurrection and victory over death and sin.

28 December

John the Baptist & Jesus

The Child Jesus continued to grow and became strong.
He was filled with wisdom and the grace of God was on Him.
(Luke 2 v 40)

The child John the Baptist also grew up and became strong in the Spirit,
and he lived in the wilderness until he appeared publicly.
(Luke 1 v 80)

The Baptist's Message:

There appeared a man, having been sent from God, his name was John.
He came as a witness, that he could testify about the Light, that
everyone may believe through him.
He was not the Light, but he would witness about the Light.

The true Light, who enlightens every person, was coming into the world.
(John 1 v 6-9)

John the Baptist' (God's) Message:

He preached the baptism of the repentance of sins:
(Luke 3 v 1-6 , Matthew 3 v 1 -6, Mark 1 v 1-5, John 1 v 32 - 34)

A voice calling in the wilderness:
"Prepare the way for the Lord, make straight the paths for the
Lord-
Fill the valleys in, make the mountains low;
The crooked roads shall become straight, the rough ways smooth.

ALL PEOPLE WILL SEE GOD'S SALVATION."

When John the Baptist first saw Jesus in person , he said:

" Look, there is the Lamb of God, who takes away the sins of the world."

(John 1 v 29)

Jesus' Message:

"The Spirit of the Lord (God) is on (in) me,
Because He has anointed me:

- To bring good news to the poor / humble
- He has sent me to heal the broken-hearted.
- To proclaim deliverance to those in captivity
- Recovery of sight to the blind
- To set free and send out in deliverance those who are oppressed

To tell everyone it's the time of the Lord's favour. (Luke 4 v 14 -21)

Jesus also said, that the 2 most important commandments are:
(Matthew 22 v 39)

1. Love the Lord your God with all your heart, soul, mind & strength;

2. Love your neighbour as (you love) yourself.

29 December

A short Nativity (Christmas) Reflection

~ John 3 v 16

During the Christmas season, many people across the world celebrate the birth of the Baby Jesus.

Furthermore, Christians across the world also look ahead to Easter (The last Passover):

During the Last Passover meal (The last supper) Jesus instituted Communion:

The bread resembles His body, and the 'vine juice' resembles His blood.

The Passover Lamb of God- Jesus Christ- was sacrificed on the cross,

as an atonement offer for each person's wrongs (sin).

In this way, God loved (Agape-perfect complete love) the world:
That He gave His only Son; So that whoever believes in Him will not be lost, but will have Eternal Life.

Because God did not send His Son into the world to judge it, But that the world would be saved through Him. (John 3 v 16,17)

An invitation to the wedding Banquet of all times!

The Gospel (Good News) of Jesus Christ ~
Son of God & Son of Mankind:

Jesus Christ entered earth as a Newborn Baby:
 in simplicity, in swaddling cloths in a manger;
Jesus as an adult:
ended life on earth (or so it seemed) as a man dying on a cross.

But thankfully for us, He also died as the Son of the Living God,
who raised Him up from the dead again on the 3rd day. Many witnessed
that & He appeared to many people alive!

After 40 days Jesus ascended to heaven, from where He is sitting at
God's right hand, victorious over death & sin, awaiting His second
coming.
Then there will be a final end to all evil and the devil (d-evil to hell)- who
always tries to destroy people's lives because he is a deceiver, a liar and
a murderer .

This is also when God will take His children to Heaven, all who have
accepted Him-where we will have no illness or suffering or sadness, just
PERFECT health, happiness, peace and Life Eternal.

There will be a Wedding Banquet in Heaven:

God sees His Church as the Bride of Christ- and as such each person
can join the wedding celebration in Heaven.
Each who accepts Jesus as His Son, and their personal Messiah
(Saviour). (Matt 22 v 1-14, Luke 14 v 15-24, Rev 19 v 6-10)

30 December

Jesus: " It is completed."

Dying on the Cross for the sins of the world, each of us, Jesus said:

"IT IS FINISHED!"
(Koine Greek: It is completed, It has been fully accomplished)
(John 19 v 30)

"Father, into Your hands, I commit (give) My spirit 'and then He died. (Luke 23 v 46)

At that very moment, the veil (curtain) of the Holy of Holies in the temple was torn in two, from top to bottom. (Matt 27 v 51)

This means:

- We ,since then and now, have access to the Holy Pure God, through Jesus.

- His blood cleanses us from ALL sin(s) and washes us as white as snow. (1 John 1 v 7, Isaiah 1 v 18)

- And we can call God, "Father":
  See what great love our Father God gives to us;
  that we are called His children; children of God- and so we are!
  (1 John 3 v 1)

Jesus invites us today to Look up to Him, dying for your and my struggles, weaknesses & sins (wrongs) on the cross, saying:

" It is done, finished; completed; sorted!

Accept My atonement & redemption for yourself
and find a fresh new start , a clean slate
and eternal life."

It can be very simple:

A criminal person, on the cross next to Jesus said:

"Jesus please remember me when you are back in Your Kingdom (Heaven)."

And Jesus said to him:

"Today you will be with Me in heaven."

PRAYER SUGGESTION:

"God, I accept that I am struggling and fall short, please forgive me-
I accept your offer of Jesus dying in my place, paying for all my debt.

Jesus,
Please wash me clean by Your blood that was shed for me,
and give me a fresh start through your Holy Spirit.

I ask this in the precious Name of Jesus

Amen (Means: This is true)

31 December

Ways to grow in FAITH:

- Share with someone who can help, that you have taken, or want to take this step.

- Read Scripture (The Bible) regularly

Jesus himself said we cannot live on earthly bread alone, but need the Words (Bread) of God too. (Luke 4 v 4)

- Join a church family (in person or online)

- Look into being baptised (Jesus Himself set the example of doing this- when we get baptised it's a sign of washing ourselves from the past, and starting afresh ~ dying from the old, and rising up to a New life.)

- Pray: 'The Our Father prayer' is always a good start:

Prayer is simply a chat , albeit with respect, to God.

It does not have to be long…

The Our Father PRAYER:

"Our Father in heaven:

Your Name be honoured,
Your Kingdom come,
Your will be done on earth, as it is in heaven.

Provide (give) for us today, our daily bread. (what we need).

Forgive us our wrongs (trespasses; sins; debt), as we forgive those who
have wronged us (or sinned against us).

Let us not come into temptation (or tempting situations);

But deliver us from evil.

Because (for) to You belong (Yours are) :

　The Kingdom,
　The Power and
　The Glory.

Forever and ever (from eternity to eternity),
AMEN.

A last thought

From Jesus' parents on earth's family lines,

We notice that God gave people the freedom of choice, hence some people even in Jesus' earthly family line, made bad choices e.g. committed things like murder or adultery;
some made good choices;
Others tried a mix of the good and the bad,
and that did not work well at all.

God has shown his faithfulness and mercy throughout the ages in reaching out to people and He still does today, as actually, Scripture tells us, as with Adam & Eve;

'All have sinned and fall short of God's glory. '(Romans 2 v 23)

Jesus' invitation still stands today for everyone & anyone to accept Him and His atonement offer; while there is still time to do so.

I invite you to put your trust in the Lion of Judah , Who has overcome ! And who is coming back soon …to take His children home to Heaven.

And he said to me:

" Do not cry,

    Look:

    The Lion, of the tribe of Judah, the root of David, has triumphed."

(Revelation 5 v 5)

About the Author & Thank You!

Thank you for taking the time to read this book.
My prayer is that you may also find encouragement & hope in what many (including myself) believe to be:

'The first and true Christmas story. The first Noel …and where it all began.

Liesel NF is a medical doctor who has worked in General medicine & in mental health, for over 30 years.

She has been a Believer since a young age.

During her extensive working career she recognised that there was, is; a big spiritual need in people. .

During the Covid pandemic she felt called by the Lord to shift her focus; studying The Holy Scriptures in depth and sharing the HOPE of the Gospel of New & Everlasting life in Jesus Christ.

This book is part of a series of books in the Life of Jesus the Saviour.

The GOOD news (Gospel) of the Coming, birth and life of the Messiah and much more …

May you be truly blessed with reading this very encouraging (true) story!

Yours faithfully,

The Author

Other books from this Author and website info

- Jesus from Manger to Ministry- This follows on from where the above book ends.

- Jesus Christ Story of His Life
(similar content to above, but in colour writing)

- Mark's Message Minuted for You
(The Good news according to Mark)

- Acts of the Apostles & Actions of the Believers
(Published Nov. 2025) All about the Holy Spirit & The Early Believers.

All available on Amazon worldwide, under ' Liesel Neatfaith" ;
soon to be available on other sites too.
(Eg Ingram Spark, Nielsen UK)

Follow us on facebook & Instagram : Neatfaith life

All the books are visible on & provide available reading pages & regular blogs on our Website:

   www.neatfaithbooks.com

Orders can be made from the above website or directly from Amazon
(and Ingram Spark soon).

We have kept costs as low as possible, so the profit margin is very low, to enable as many people as possible, affordable access to the books.

We also give 10 % of all profits to charitable causes.

Be blessed !

Space for personal reflection notes or prayers:

Which passage spoke most to you in this book?

Would you like to jot down a prayer to Jesus , The Saviour to the world:

Printed in Dunstable, United Kingdom